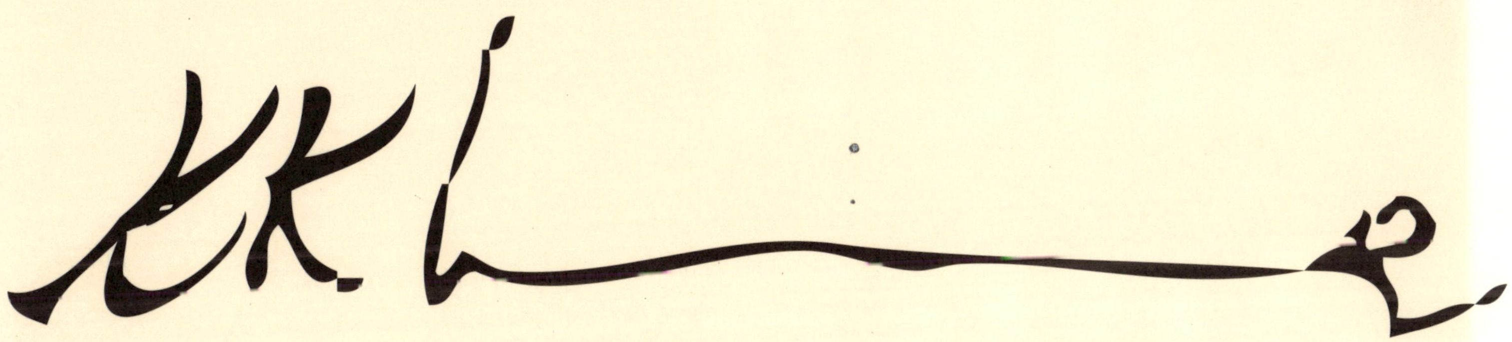

Krishen Khanna
Chola Migrations

Photography by Karan Khanna | Designed by Revanta Sarabhai | Produced and Published by Mapin Publishing | www.mapinpub.com

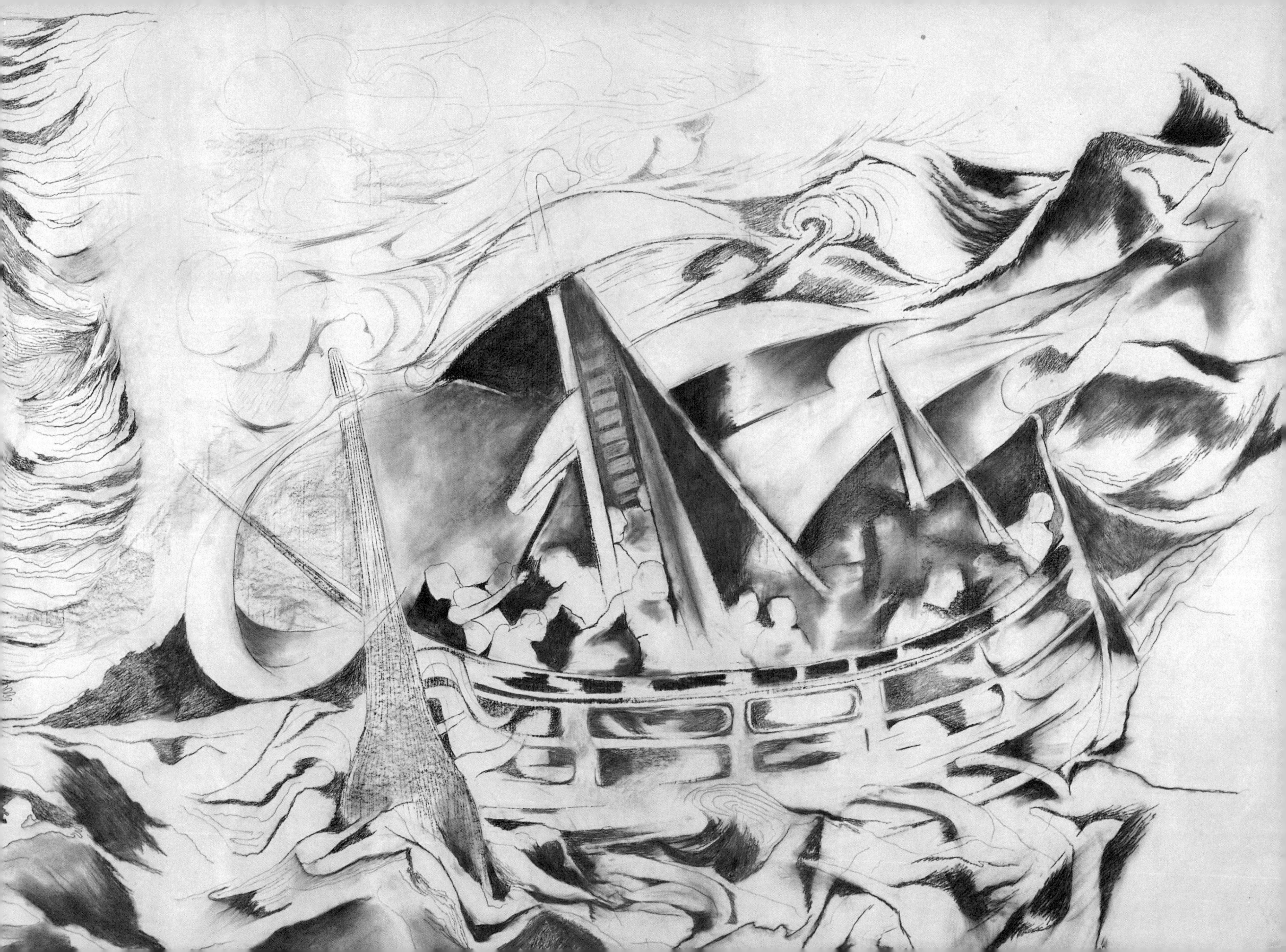

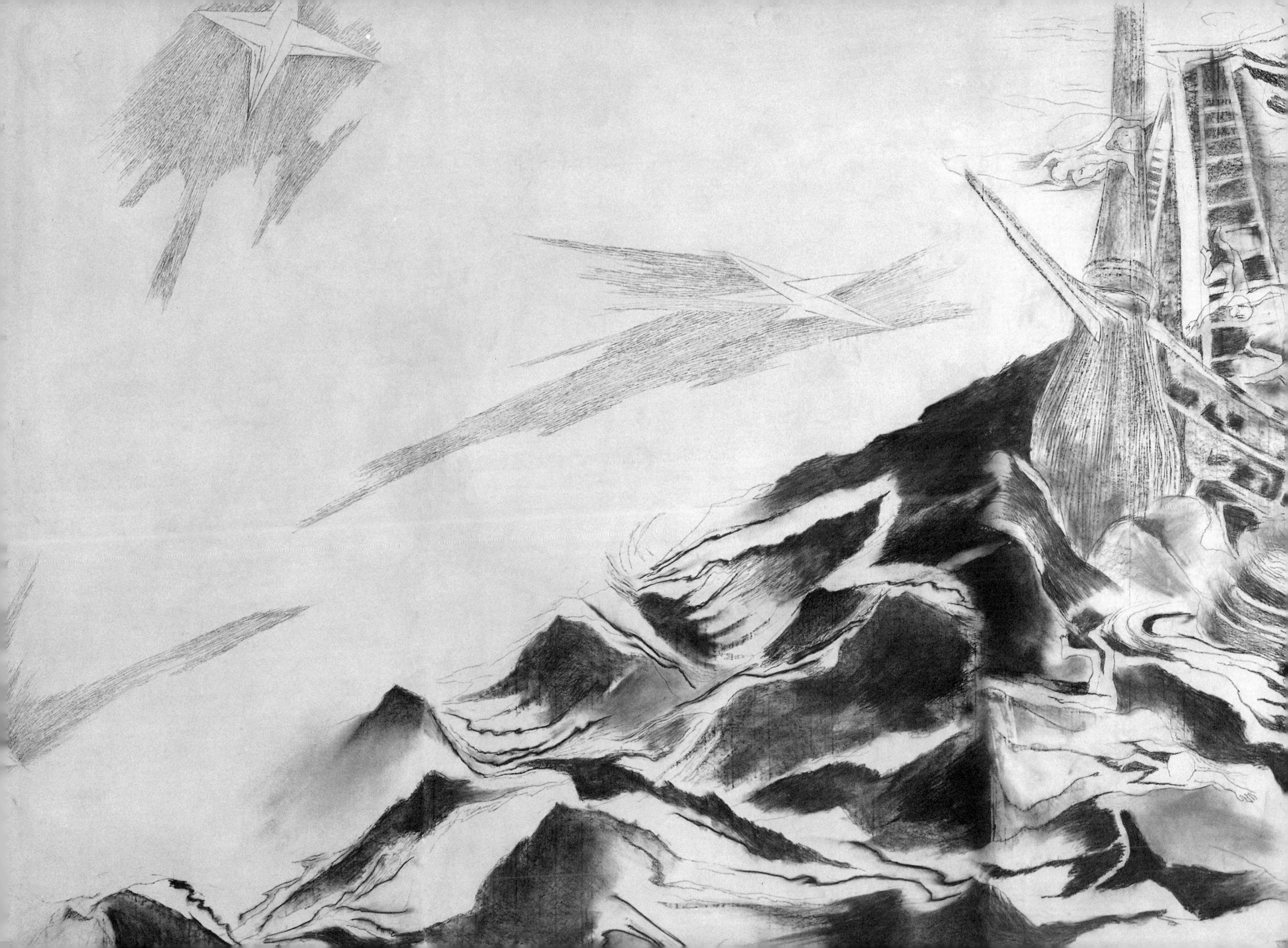

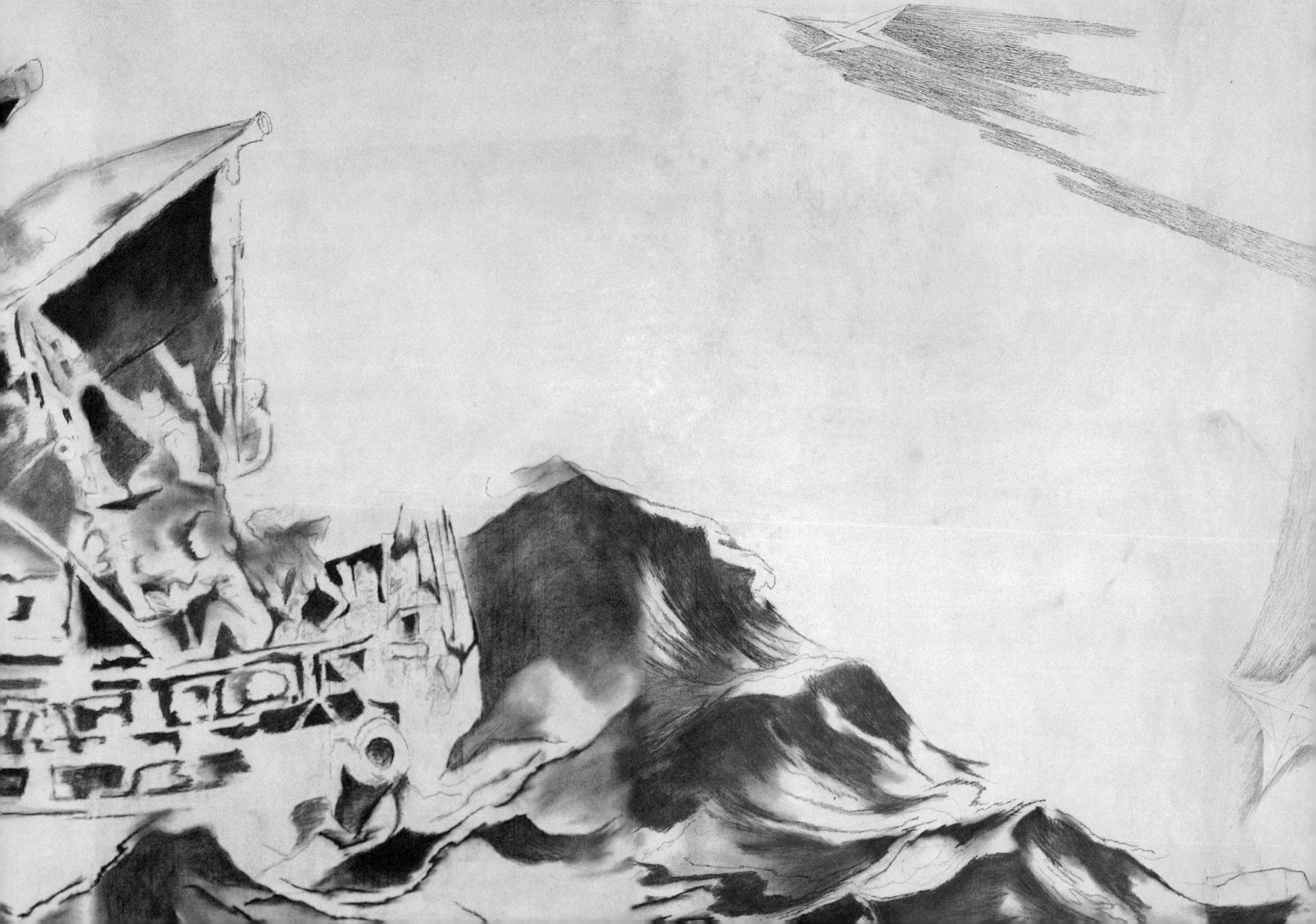

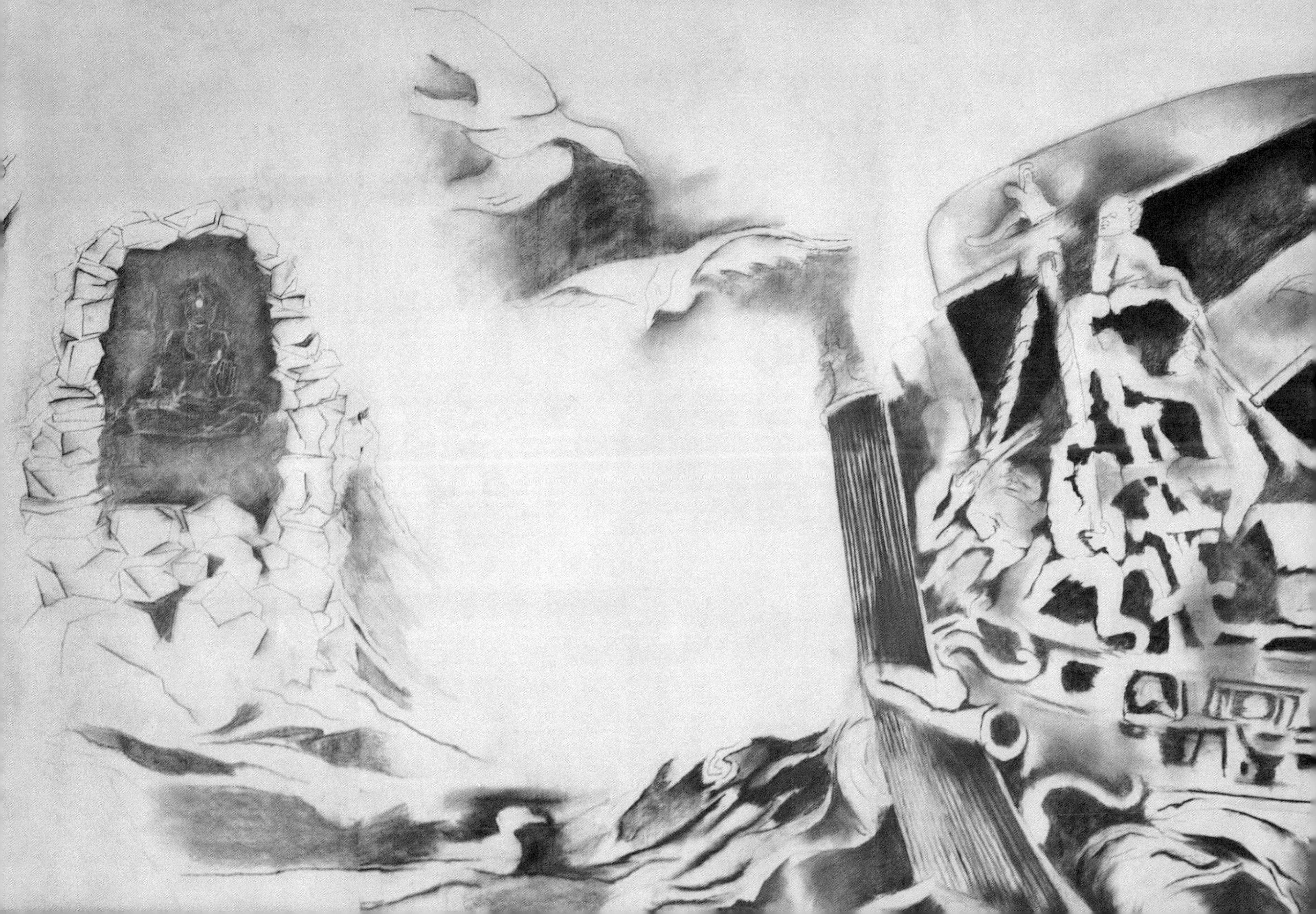

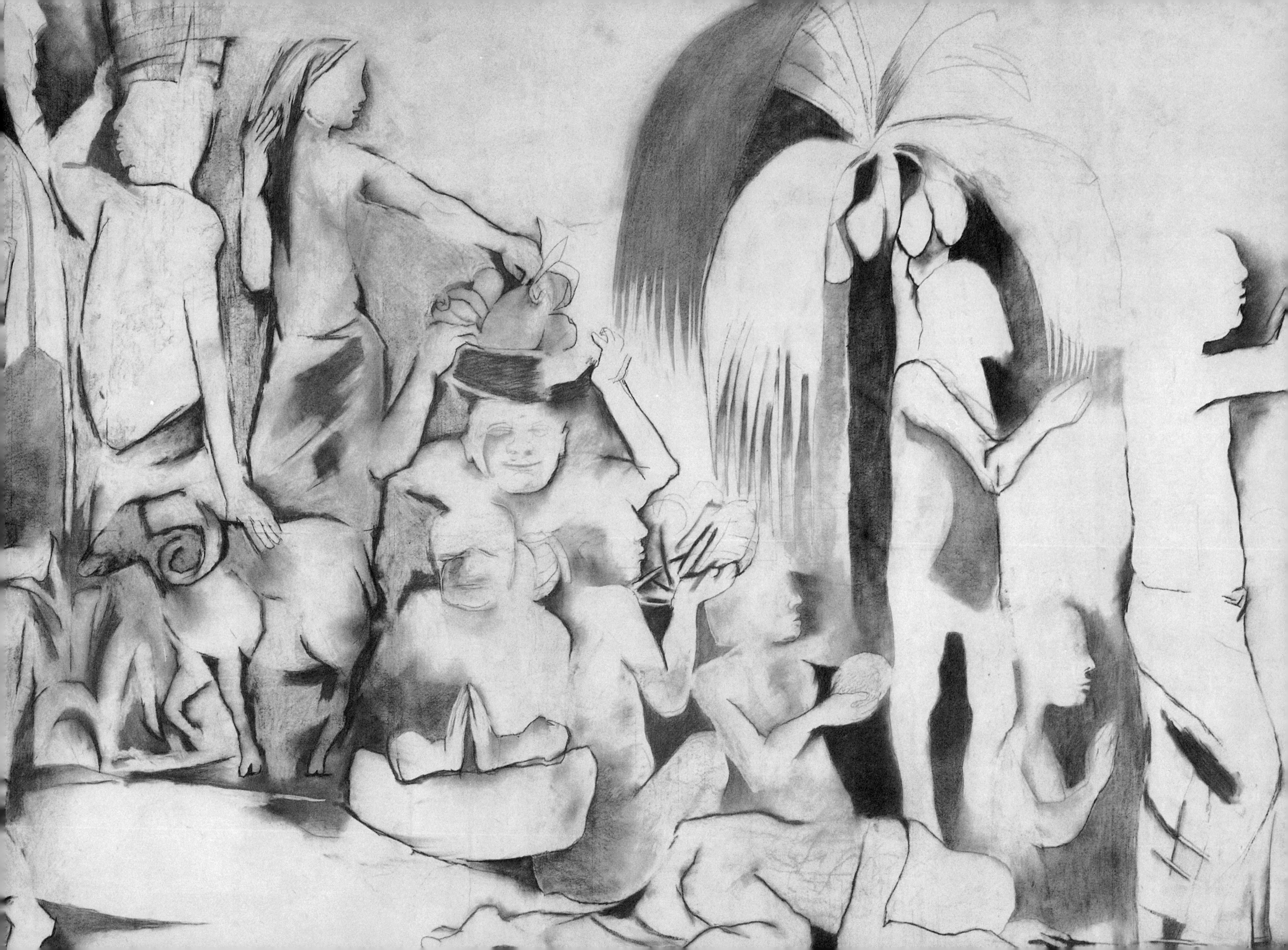

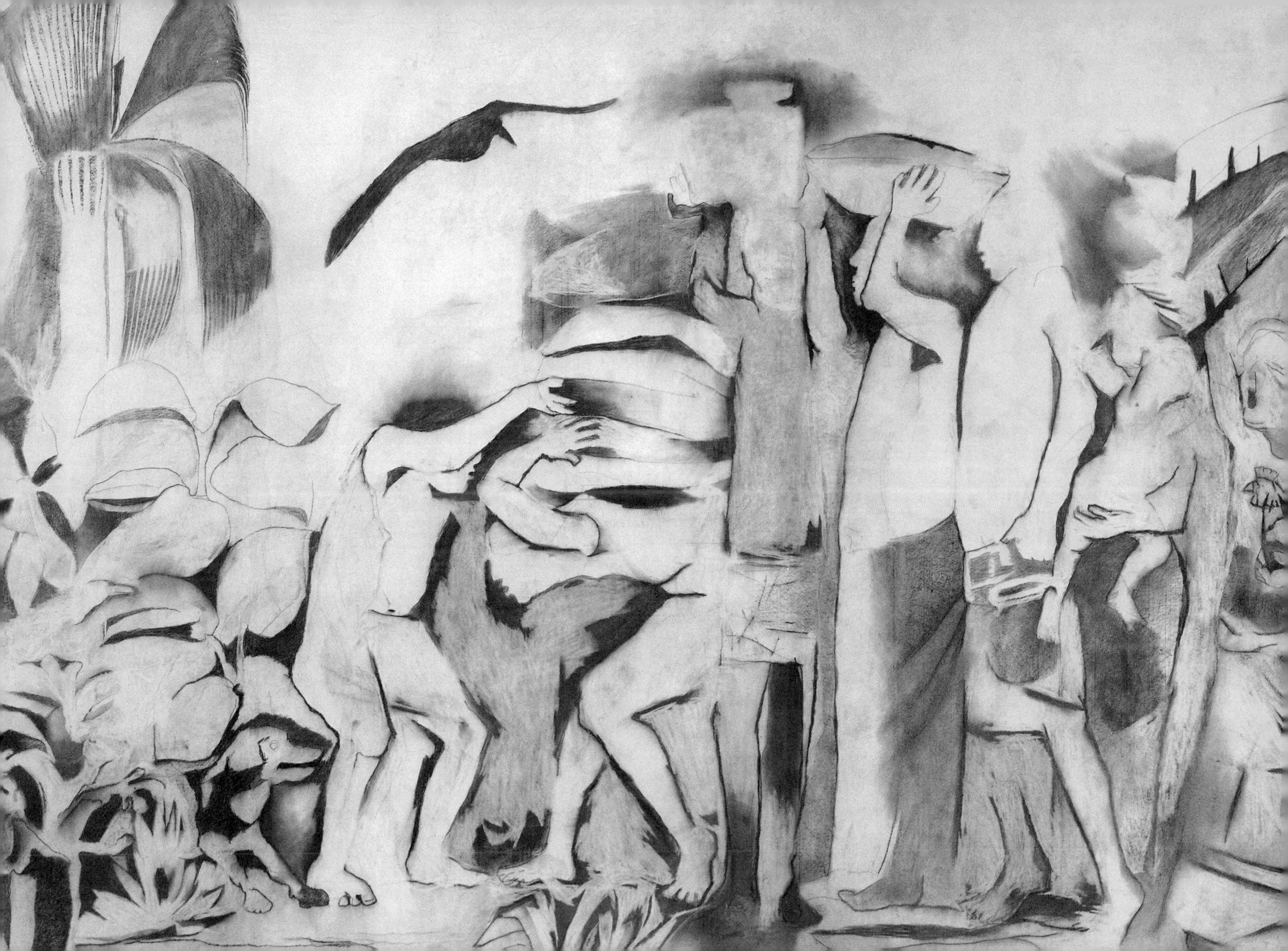

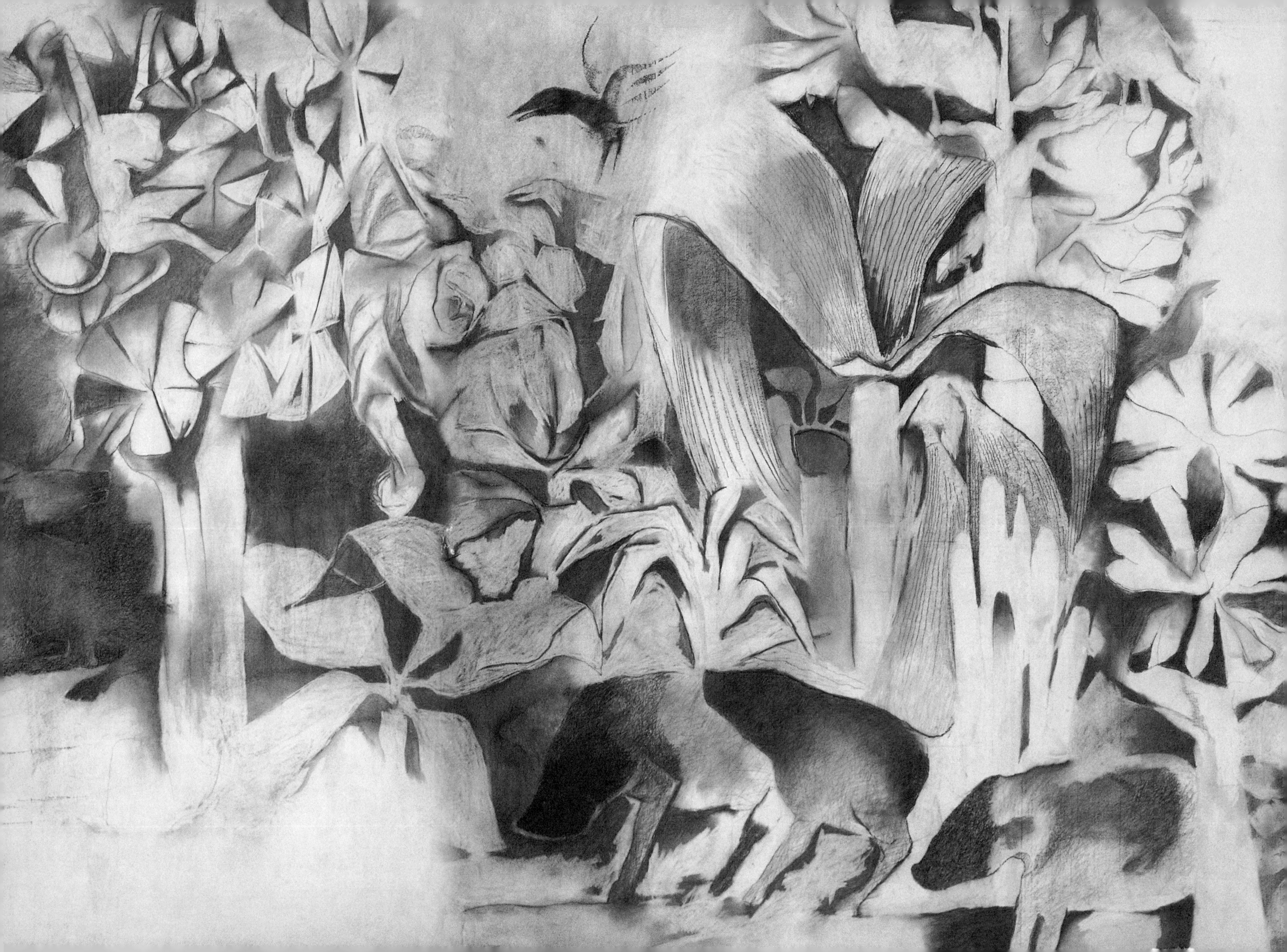

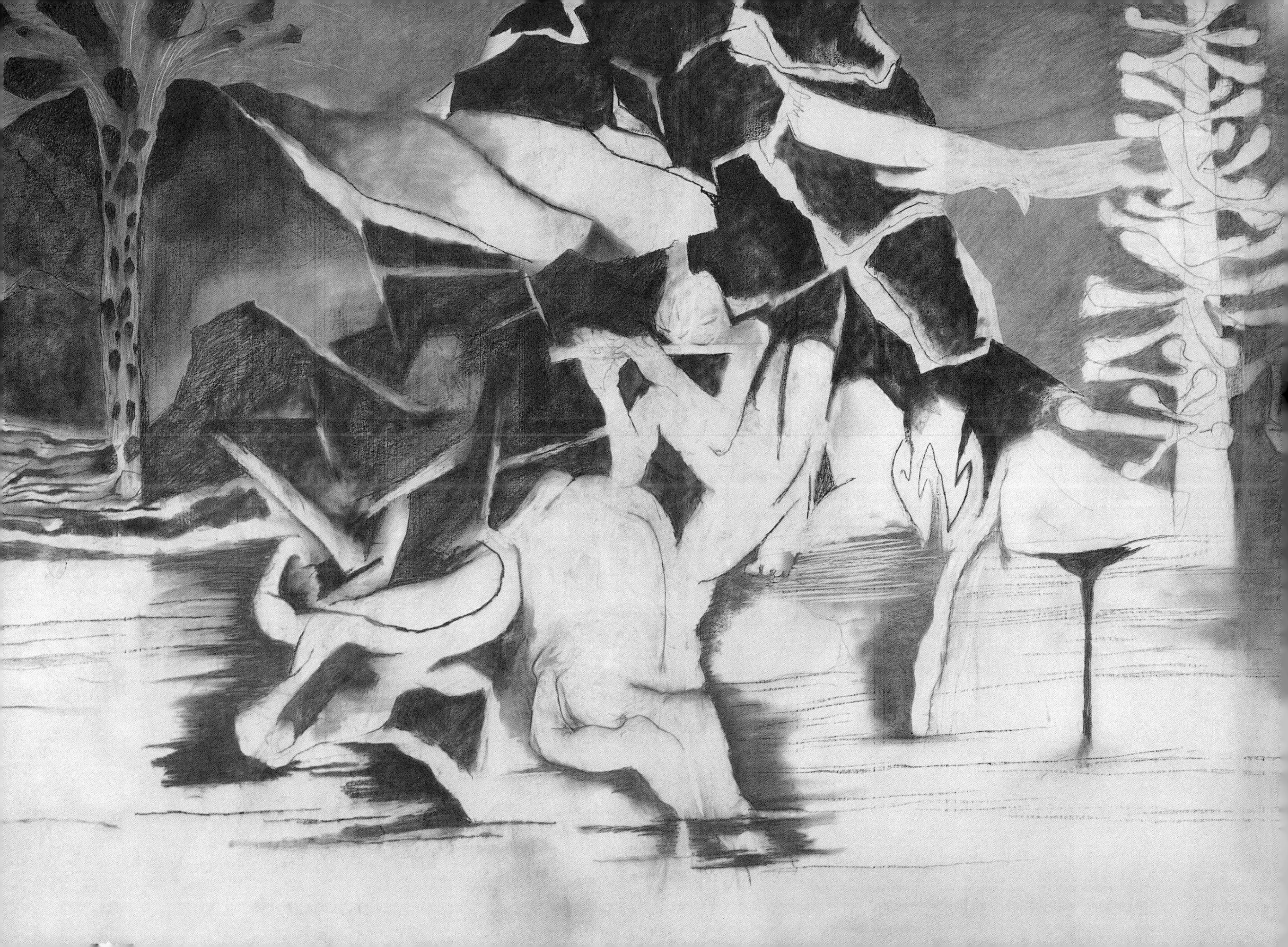